FREDDIE
and the
Ten Commandments

A Series Based on the Ten Commandments

By
BARBARA L. WILLIAMS

Illustrated by
Howard Moore

ACKNOWLEDGEMENT

The illustrations in this book were furnished by Mr.
Howard Moore, Christian artist, of Los Angeles, California.
Mr. Moore was formerly an artist with Walt Disney Films,
Inc., of California.

CONTENTS

AUTHOR'S PREFACE

The following is a group of ten stories based on the Ten Commandments. The purpose of the stories is to illustrate and explain the commandments in terms and incidents familiar to the beginner or primary child. This series endeavors to help the child understand and apply the Ten Commandments to his own life.

Parents will find these stories useful in the home training of their children. They may be used as devotional or bedtime stories. **Freddie and the Ten Commandments** will enrich any child's library.

Sunday School teachers, Christian day school teachers, camp leaders and Vacation Bible School teachers will all find this book valuable as an aid in teaching the Ten Commandments. The ten stories will fit into a ten day program or they may be grouped together to make a shorter series.

It is the author's desire and prayer that **Freddie and the Ten Commandments** will develop in many of God's little ones a clearer understanding of the Ten Commandments and thus lead many to a closer relationship with their Heavenly Father.

The Author

FOREWORD

It has given me a great deal of pleasure to have read the manuscript for this book by Miss Barbara Williams and to have encouraged her in this work.

Good books and proper Christian literature is one of the most important aspects of training children in the way of right living. Possibly no other influence outside that of the parents themselves is more powerful upon a child's life than that he sees in print. The story book has the advantage of the child's going back to it again and again until the material has become "set" in his mind. It is hardly possible to give a child too many good books to read.

This book will make a fine contribution toward Christian child training in the home. I take pleasure in commending it to our many friends, especially among the younger couples with children, and to the reading public. It fills a need for giving the child a proper appreciation of the Law of God and should be read by millions of American children.

Miss Williams was formerly librarian of Western Pilgrim College, El Monte, California for several years, where the writer was privileged to be associated with her as President of the college. She has always proved herself a devout and consistent Christian worker. A native of southern Oregon, she was early converted to Christ and has spent almost her entire life in Christian circles and much of it in Christian work. This is her first book but we trust it is only the beginning of a successful work in the field of Christian writing.

William S. Deal

FREDDIE'S PRESENT

"Thou shalt have no other gods before me."—Exodus 20:3.

FREDDIE Brooks awoke suddenly and sat up in bed. The bright sunshine was coming in his window. He jumped out of bed, dressed, and ran down stairs. Today was Saturday and his fifth birthday. He was anxious to see what Daddy and Mother had for him.

"Happy Birthday," his mother and father called as he landed on the bottom step.

Freddie ran to look where his mother usually put his present. All he found was a card. On the card it said, "Look by the stove." Running over to the stove he saw a box. In it something was moving. There he found a cute, little black puppy.

"Bow-wow," barked the puppy as it jumped into Freddie's arms.

"Thank you, thank you, Mother and Daddy!" cried Freddie with delight. "I am going to call him Blackie." After breakfast, Freddie and Blackie went out to play in the warm sunshine. Freddie was very happy to have someone to play with as he did not have any brothers or sisters.

That night Freddie said his prayers, went to bed, and was soon fast asleep. He had played hard with Blackie and was very tired.

The next morning after Freddie had eaten breakfast, he wanted to play with his puppy. Just as he picked up Blackie, his mother called, "Freddie, it is time to get ready for Sunday School. Freddie had forgotten all about Sunday School. He always went to Sunday School and church with his parents.

Freddie wanted to play with his puppy so badly that he decided he would not go to Sunday School. "I am not going," he answered.

"What? You're not going to Sunday School?" asked his mother.

"No, I am going to stay home and play with Blackie."

"But you m u s t go to Sunday School," said mother.

Then Freddie began to whine and cry, hoping his mother would let him stay home.

Just then his father came into the room. "What is all this fussing about?" he asked.

"Why can't I stay home and play with Blackie?" cried Freddie.

"Let's look into God's Word to see if it will tell us why you shouldn't stay home and play with your puppy," said his father. He picked up the

Bible and sat down with Freddie. Opening the Bible to Exodus 20:3 he read, "Thou shalt have no other gods before me." "That is the first commandment that God gave His people," Freddie's father said. "Do you know what it means?"

"No" said Freddie, who had stopped crying. "What does that have to do with my puppy?"

" 'Thou shalt have no other gods before me' means that we should love God more than we love anything else," his father explained. "It means we should love Him so much that we will do just what He wants us to do. Anything that will keep us from doing what God wants can become a god that we put before our true God. These other gods may be things like toys, money, people, and your cute little black puppy," his father said. "You should go to Sunday School instead of playing with the puppy because you love God more than you love Blackie."

"Oh, I see," said Freddie. "I love God, so I will go to Sunday School." He jumped up and ran upstairs to get ready.

In this way, Freddie learned the meaning of the first commandment.

A LETTER FROM AUNT MARY

"Thou Shalt Not Make Unto thee Any Graven Image."—Exodus 20:4

"FREDDIE", called Mother, as Freddie was going down the driveway in his wagon. "Please bring me the mail."

Freddie got out of the wagon and ran to the mailbox. Standing on tiptoes he reached into the mailbox and pulled out a letter. Then he ran to the house.

"Just one letter, Mother," he called. Mother stepped out on the porch and took the letter.

Freddie was going back to his wagon when she called, "Come here a minute, Freddie. This letter is addressed to Mr. Freddie Lee Brooks." "That's me!" exclaimed Freddie with joy. "Who is it from? What does it say? Read it to me!"

"Just a minute," said his mother. "One question at a time. It is from Mrs. Mary Johnson. That is your Aunt Mary. Let's open it now and see what it says."

Freddie took the letter and excitedly tore it open, took the pages out and looked at them. "Read it, Mother, please."

His mother took the letter and read, "Dear Freddie, I would like to have you visit me and stay a whole week. Ask your mother if you can come a week from Monday. Love, Aunt Mary."

Freddie jumped up and down happily. "May I go, Mother?" he pleaded.

"Yes, Freddie, I think you may go. We will ask your father tonight."

That night when Freddie showed the letter to his father, his father told him he could stay a whole week with Aunt Mary.

Freddie could hardly wait for his

father to take him to Aunt Mary's house. Each day he was more excited as he longed for the time to come. At last the day came. Mr. Brooks took Freddie in the family car to Aunt Mary's house. He kissed him good-bye and soon left for home.

Each day Freddie seemed to have more fun than the d a y before. Auntie, as Freddie called her, took him to see many things in her city— the fire station, the train station, the museum, and many other places. One day they even invited some other small boys over to play games and have a party.

On Sunday evening a missionary came to Aunt Mary's church and showed missionary pictures. In these pictures Freddie saw people bowing down to huge and very ugly statues called idols and worshipping them. The people brought gifts and laid them at the idol's feet. After praying to the idol, they left looking very sad and unhappy. "I am going to ask Daddy to tell me more about these idols," thought Freddie.

Freddie could hardly wait until his father came for him. Although he had a good time, he wanted to be home again. His father came early Monday morning. They said good-bye to Auntie and started home. One of the first questions Freddie asked his father was about the idols he had seen in the pictures.

"What are idols and why don't we have them?" Freddie asked.

"Well," said his father, "those idols are images of the people's idea of God. They make the statues or idols and worship them. But God wants us to pray to Him and not to idols. Our God is the living God who can answer our prayers. It does not please God when we make graven images and pray to them."

"But, Daddy," asked Freddie, "how do we know that God does not want them to worship those idols?"

"The second commandment that God gave His people in the Old Testament was, 'Thou shalt not make unto thee any graven image . . .' He also told them not to bow down to the images. God wants us to worship Him and not anything or anyone else."

"I am glad that we pray to God," said Freddie, "because He hears us and can help us. The idols they worship can not do anything."

A NEW PLAYMATE

"Thou shalt not take the name of the Lord Thy God In Vain."—Exodus 20:7

ARLY one morning, Freddie glanced out his window. He saw a big truck pull up in front of the house across the street. Behind it he saw a car drive up. As he watched, he decided that some new people were moving in. Just then a boy about his age, jumped out of the car.

"Oh, boy!" exclaimed Freddie, "I'll have someone to play with!" Freddie ran to tell his mother. "Some people are moving in across the street, and they have a boy!" he cried excitedly.

"May I go watch?"

"Yes, you may watch from the window," said his mother, "but I don't think you ought to go out right now.

It is chilly, and besides, you might get in the way."

Disappointed, Freddie went into the living room to gaze at the people moving in. Soon he forgot his disappointment as he watched the moving men move the things out of the big truck and into the house.

Later in the day, Freddie saw the little boy in the yard. He wanted to find out his name and play with him.

He went into the kitchen where his mother was doing dishes. "May I go out and play with the new boy?" he asked.

"You may go see if he may come over and play in the back yard," his mother answered.

Out of the house and across the street ran Freddie. "Hi!" he said to the boy. "My name is Freddie. What is yours?"

"Bob", he answered bashfully.

Before Freddie and Bob had talked

very long, Bob got over his bashful-
ness. After asking Bob's mother if
he could play in Freddie's yard, Freddie showed Bob his swing and his
puppy, Blackie.

The two little boys played for a
long while. They p l a y e d with
Blackie, swung, and played tag. Once
when Bob fell out of the swing he
swore, using God's name.

When Freddie asked Bob why he
said it, he answered "The moving
man says it when he gets mad. Once
the piano slipped and hit his toe and
he said it."

A little later Bob fell down and
again he used God's name. This time
Freddie's mother heard him and
called the boys. She told them that
it was not right to use God's name in
that manner.

"Why?" asked Bob. "The moving
man does it."

"The moving man should not do

it," said Freddie's mother. "The Bible tells us it is not pleasing to God to swear and use God's or Jesus' name like that. The third commandment is, 'Thou shalt not take the name of the Lord, thy God in vain.' "

After Bob had gone home, Freddie's mother asked him if Bob used God's name in vain any more.

"No," answered Freddie.

"I am glad," said his mother. "I want you to have a nice playmate, but not one who will swear when anything happens that he doesn't like."

Freddie was very happy when he crawled into bed that night. He was glad that he had a new playmate, but more than that he was glad that his new friend had learned not to use God's name in vain.

FREDDIE'S WORK

"Remember The Sabbath Day, To Keep It Holy." —Exodus 20:8

ONE Saturday before his father went to work, he said, "Freddie, if you clean the yard, I will take you and Bob to the zoo next Monday. But, if it isn't done you will have to stay home and clean it."

"Oh, goody!" exclaimed Freddie, "I will do it."

When Bob came over to play that morning, Freddie told him that they were going to get to go to the zoo.

"But I have to clean the yard first," he explained.

"It is a long time until Monday," said Bob. "You will have plenty of time to do that."

So the boys played happily while thinking of the good time they would have at the zoo. But each time they thought of cleaning the yard, they decided they had plenty of time and would do it later.

Saturday afternoon came and still the yard was not clean. Freddie's mother knew what his father had told him, so she decided to talk to Freddie about it. "Freddie, you will have to hurry if you get the yard cleaned before it gets dark. You want to go to the zoo, don't you?"

"Oh, I'll help you and we can do it tomorrow," said Bob, who was standing near.

"But tomorrow is Sunday, and we do not work on Sunday," replied Freddie's mother. "That is the Lord's day."

Bob looked puzzled, as his parents did everything on Sunday that they did on other days.

"God wouldn't care if we just cleaned the yard tomorrow afternoon, would He?" asked Freddie. "I can still go to Sunday School in the morning."

"You know better than that," said his mother. "But I do not think Bob does. Would you like to know why we don't work or do some of the other things on Sunday that we do on other days, Bob?"

"Yes," replied Bob, "I don't understand. Sunday is just the same as any other day at our house."

"I am afraid it is at most houses," said Mrs. Brooks. "But God tells us in His Word that Sunday should not be like other days. Freddie, can you quote the fourth commandment for Bob?"

"Remember the sabbath day, to keep it holy," quoted Freddie.

"And in another place it tells us not to do any work on the sabbath because it is the Lord's Day. We should keep it holy unto God," said Freddie's mother.

"Is that why you always go to Sunday School on Sunday?" asked Bob.

"Yes," answered Freddie. "That is one way we can keep it holy. Why don't you go with us?"

"I think I will," said Bob. "I want to learn about God and His commandments, too."

"Well, I had better hurry and get the yard cleaned so we can go to the zoo, Monday," said Freddie.

"I will help," offered Bob, as the boys hurried to get the yard cleaned.

On Sunday both boys went to Sunday School to learn about God. Bob enjoyed it and decided to go every Sunday.

Early Monday morning they went to the zoo and had a wonderful time.

Freddie's father and both the boys were happy that they had cleaned the yard on Saturday and had kept Sunday holy.

A BALL GAME

"Honour Thy Father And Thy Mother."—Exodus 20:12.

"**M**AY I go out and play, Mother?" Freddie asked.

"You may go outside and play if you stay in the yard," Mrs. Brooks replied.

"All right, I will stay in the yard," said Freddie as he went out the door.

For a long time Freddie played by himself in the yard. Then he saw some other boys coming up the street with a bat, a ball, and a glove. Freddie went to the gate to talk to them.

"Where are you going?" he asked.

"We are going up the street to the vacant lot to play ball. Why don't you come along?" they answered.

"I can't" said Freddie, "Mother told me to stay in the yard."

"Oh, come on for just a little while,"

pleaded one of the boys. "Your mother is busy and won't miss you."

Freddie knew that he should not go, but he was tired of playing alone. "A game of ball would be fun," he thought. "I'll just stay a little while." So he climbed over the fence and joined the boys.

Soon the boys were in the middle of a ball game having lots of fun. All but Freddie, that is. Somehow he could not keep his mind on the game. He knew that he had disobeyed his mother and that she would be unhappy about it.

He remembered a commandment he had learned in Sunday School. "Honour thy father and thy mother." "That means that we should love, respect, and obey our parents. We should trust them and do what they say because they are wiser and know best," the teacher had taught him.

By the time the ball game was

over, Freddie was feeling very badly. He walked home slowly. He did not want to see his mother for he knew that he had disobeyed her and would be punished. He also knew that he had broken one of God's commandments, and God was displeased with him.

By the time he reached home he was almost crying. As soon as he saw his mother, he ran to her. "I'm sorry," he sobbed, "I won't go away again when I am not supposed to!"

His mother was sad because Freddie had disobeyed her, but she knew that he had learned a good lesson. She also knew that he would remember better next time if he was punished, so she gave him a spanking and made him stay in his room the rest of the afternoon.

After that Freddie remembered that it was best to honour his father and mother, as the commandment says.

A BIBLE STORY

"Thou Shalt Not Kill."—Exodus 20:-
13.

"Tell me a story, Mother," begged Freddie one day when he was sick and had to stay in bed.

"All right," said his mother. "Would you like to hear a Bible story about a man who broke the commandment, 'Thou shalt not kill'?"

"Yes," said Freddie. "Did he live a long time ago?"

"He lived a very long time ago," replied Mrs. Brooks. "In fact the story is about the first two sons of the first man and woman, Adam and Eve. The boys' names were Cain and Abel."

"That will be interesting," exclaimed Freddie.

"Cain was a man who made his living from the ground like farmers do today," his mother started the story. "Abel made his living by keeping sheep. When it came time to give an offering to the Lord, Abel brought his best lamb and gave it to God. But Cain brought an offering from the things that he had grown. God was pleased with Abel's offering because it was a live offering, but Cain's offering did not please Him.

"Cain was jealous and angry because Abel's offering was accepted and his wasn't. One day as the two brothers were in the field Cain killed his brother.

"Later God asked Cain, 'Where is Abel, your brother?'

"Cain answered, 'I do not know.'

"God knew that Cain had killed his brother, Abel. So to punish him He told Cain that he would not have a home any more. He would wander from place to place. God sent Cain out from His presence. Cain lived like the beggars and the bums we have today who wander around from place to place.

"That is how God punished the first one who broke the commandment, 'Thou shalt not kill' ", mother told Freddie.

A SUNDAY SCHOOL LESSON

"Thou Shalt Not Commit Adultery."
—Exodus 20:14.

AS Freddie and his new friend, Bob entered the boys' Sunday School classroom they saw a flannelgraph board with a figure of a man on it.

"Today," the teacher began, "we are going to study about the seventh commandment, 'Thou shalt not commit adultery.' Adultery is a big word for little boys. Does anyone know what this commandment means?"

"Does it have something to do with a woman and a man?" asked one of the boys, looking at the man on the flannelgraph board.

"Yes," said the teacher. "In a family there is one man, one woman and the children." The teacher then put a figure of a woman and a couple of children next to the man.

" 'Thou shalt not commit adultery' means that one man and one woman should live together as man and wife, with their children. The members of the family love each other more than people outside the family. This is God's plan. If the man in this family should love another woman besides his wife, he would be disobeying God, or, if the woman should love another man, she would be disobeying God.

"Do you remember Johnny, the boy who used to be in our class? He went to live with his grandmother."

"I do," said several of the boys who had been Johnny's friends.

"Does anyone know why Johnny had to go live with his grandmother?"

"Because his daddy went away and did not come back," said Freddie. Johnny had been a good friend of Freddie's.

"Yes," said the teacher. "Johnny's father decided he loved another woman more than Johnny's mother. He left Johnny and his mother and went to another town to live with this other woman. Johnny's father disobeyed t h e seventh commandment," the teacher explained.

"Johnny was very sad and unhappy when his daddy did not come back," said Freddie.

"Yes," the teacher replied. "When we do not keep God's laws we are unhappy and make others unhappy.

"God made the family so that children would have one mother and one father. In this way parents and children can live together, love and help each other to be happy," the teacher told them.

COOKIES

"Thou Shalt Not Steal."—Exodus 20:15.

ONE day Freddie was playing over at Bob's house. Bob's mother had gone to the store for a few minutes. Before she left she had made some cookies which she left cooling on the kitchen table.

It was late in the afternoon and Bob and Freddie were hungry. The cookies looked real g o o d. They wanted some very badly.

Bob said, "Let's each eat a cookie."

"Will your mother care?" asked Freddie.

"I don't know," said Bob. "But if we eat them before she gets back, she'll not know."

So each of the boys ate a big cookie and then continued playing. Bob's mother came home from the store and told Freddie it was time to go home for supper.

Freddie went home, but when he sat down to the table he just wasn't hungry.

"You aren't eating very much," said father. "Are you sick, or have you been eating before supper?"

"Oh, I ate a cookie over at Bob's house." replied Freddie.

"That is funny," said his mother, "Bob's mother wouldn't give you boys cookies so close to meal time. Did Bob's mother give it to you?" she asked.

"No," said Freddie hesitantly, "we ate it while she was gone to the store."

"Those cookies did not belong to you," said his father. "To take things which do not belong to you is stealing. Remember, God said, 'Thou shalt not steal.' "

"I think you had better go over and tell Bob's mother that you are sorry you ate that cookie," said his mother. "Next time you boys had better ask before you eat cookies."

"But," said Freddie, "Bob's mother might spank him for getting into the cookies."

"Well, maybe she won't this time. But Bob should learn that to take things that do not belong to him is breaking the commandment, 'Thou shalt not steal.' "

So Freddie went to tell Bob's mother that he was sorry, and to explain to Bob that it is not right to take what does not belong to you.

THE BROKEN VASE

"Thou Shalt Not Bear False Witness Against Thy Neighbor."—Exodus 20:16.

"**F**REDDIE, be sure you straighten up your room. You are going to have visitors today," called his mother.

"Who is coming?" asked Freddie.

"Your cousins, Susy and Sandy," his mother explained.

"Oh, good!" said Freddie. "Will they be here soon?"

Just then a car drove into the driveway and out jumped the three-year-old twin girls. They had come to spend the day with Freddie.

Freddie showed the girls his toys and helped them play with them. After they got tired of playing with the toys, Freddie decided it would be fun to play hide-and-seek with Susy and Sandy. He told them to stay in the bedroom while he hid in the living room.

"I'll hide behind the davenport," he thought. But just as he was ducking behind it, his foot hit the stand next to it.

Crash! went his mother's pretty vase to the floor.

"Oh! Oh! I'll get a spanking when mother finds it," thought Freddie. So he jumped up and ran into the bedroom.

"Let's color in my color book," he said. "I don't want to play hide-and-seek."

"All right," said Sandy as the three sat down to color.

Just then Freddie's mother who had been washing clothes decided to see how the children were getting along. When she reached the living room she saw her pretty vase broken all over the living room floor. "My best vase!" she exclaimed. "It's broken! Freddie! Come here this minute!"

When Freddie came into the room she asked, "How did my vase get broken?"

Freddie did not know what to say. "She will really be mad at me if she knows I broke it," he thought. "The twins are so little that she won't care as much. She won't spank them, but she will me."

"The twins knocked it off and it broke," said Freddie.

"No, we didn't" said the twins who had followed Freddie into the room.

"They did do it, Mother," Freddie insisted.

None of the children would say that he had broken the vase. Finally Freddie's mother decided she would spank all three of them. "They were probably playing rough and knocked it off," she thought. So all three children received a spanking. This made Sandy and Susy cry.

Freddie felt badly because it was all his fault. The more he thought about it the worse he felt. Finally, he decided he had better tell his mother that he had broken the vase.

"Mother, I broke the vase. The twins were in the bedroom when I kicked the stand with my foot and the vase fell off, I'm sorry," he sobbed.

"But why did you not say so in the first place?" asked his mother. "You told me that Susy and Sandy broke it. That was a lie. Remember the commandment, 'Thou shalt not bear false witness against thy neighbor'? To bear false witness means to lie and tell something that is not true. All those around you are your neighbors. That is exactly what you did," she explained.

"I'm sorry I did it, Mother. I'll not do it again," Freddie promised. Then he went and asked the twins to forgive him.

A SHETLAND PONY

"Thou Shalt Not Covet."—Exodus 20:17.

ONE day Freddie received an invitation. It said, "Tomorrow is my sixth birthday. I'm going to have a party. You are invited. Please come. Your cousin, Joan."

So the next day Freddie went to Joan's house to the party. After the children played games and had ice cream and cake, it was time for Joan to receive her gifts. As she was opening each of her presents, Freddie thought, "I wish I had that toy. She has so many."

"You have one m o r e present, Joan," said her mother. "It is outside."

"What could it be that is outside?" asked Joan. All her friends wondered, too.

They all went into the back yard to see. Standing by the fence was a pretty Shetland Pony.

"Oh!" exclaimed Joan in surprise. "A pony! I am so glad!"

The rest of the afternoon was spent riding the pony. All the children had a ride on it. The more Freddie looked at it, the more he wished it was his. Finally, as it was late, all of the children went home.

When Freddie arrived home, his mother asked him about the party. All he could talk about was the pony. Then he started to cry.

"What is the matter, honey?" asked his mother.

"I want that pony: I wish it were mine," Freddie sobbed.

"But it is not yours," said his mother. "It belongs to Joan."

"I know, but I want it!" cried Freddie.

"It is not right for you to want

something which belongs to someone
else. 'Thou shalt not covet' is the
last commandment. To covet means
to desire that which belongs to someone else. You had better quit crying
and forget about the pony. You want
to please God, do you not?"

"Yes," said Freddie, wiping his
eyes. "I won't cry any more. Do you
think Joan will let me ride the pony
once in a while, Mother?"

"I am sure she will," answered his
mother.

With this Freddie went to his room
to prepare for dinner.

After dinner Freddie said, "Mother, I think that I have finally learned
what all the ten commandments
mean."

"That is fine, Freddie," said his
mother, "and what do you think they
mean?"

"Well," said Freddie, "what you do
should always please God and should

not harm anyone else or take anything from him."

"Yes, Freddie, I think you have
learned them very well. If you always do this throughout your life,
you will always be happy and make
other people happy too," said his
mother as she pulled him up to her
and kissed him.

"I am going to try, mother," promised Freddie as he got a book for a
story before going to bed.

The End